The
of Cl
is Je
only way?

CHRISTIANITY'S central assertion is that God has uniquely visited our planet in the form of Jesus of Nazareth, and that by Jesus' teaching, character, life, claims, miracles, death and resurrection, he has established himself as the definitive revelation of God and the only way for us to be brought into an eternal relationship with God.

Most sceptics have traditionally argued that these Christian claims are false, but in doing so they assume they know what the truth of these matters is, because just as the phenomenon of blindness assumes the existence of sight, and evil presumes a standard of goodness, so the sceptics' cry of "error" presupposes the existence of truth, which means that

sceptics need to substantiate their own position. But this has not been done with any consistency or coherence. This difficulty is therefore sidestepped by critics of religion (Christianity in particular) by avoiding a right versus wrong approach and adopting a relativistic view.

Our increasingly relativistic society is as likely to call Christianity arrogant and intolerant as it is to suggest it is false. For many people, Christians who claim to know absolute truth about the way to God appear to come across as intolerant and arrogant. Surely, in our multi-faith society with its many religious beliefs, the only way to promote tolerance is to agree that all beliefs are only relatively true, that something is "true for me", but not necessarily "true for you".

You may well feel that Christians must stop once and for all claiming to know absolute truth about how we can come into a relationship with God and simply allow each person to do it in their own way. To get to grips with this mix of ideas we need to disentangle three distinct ingredients, which are often presented together.

Pluralism, tolerance and relativism

Pluralism At a basic sociological level, pluralism can be used as a purely descriptive word to refer to a plurality of people and ethnic groups, eg in our major cities, who represent a number of the world's religions.

Tolerance A plurality of religious beliefs creates great scope for intolerance and friction. While some people see tolerance as the only virtue, Christians for their part should acknowledge that all people are made in the image of God and therefore deserve acceptance, respect and courtesy, regardless of their religious beliefs.

Relativism In the area of values and religious beliefs, relativism claims that no absolute truth exists. Belief is strictly relative to a person's background and

perspective and not relative to objective truth. If you were born in Thailand to Buddhist parents you are likely to be Buddhist, if you were born in the American mid-west to Christian parents you are likely to be a Christian and if you were born in Iran, you are likely to be a Muslim. Given that religious truth is relative to a person's place of birth, it is thought to be intolerant and arrogant to offer our moral or religious beliefs as public (universal) truth.

Reality check

We can of course know certain things truly. I can know that today, as I type this, is Friday and tomorrow is Saturday. On the strength of tomorrow being Saturday, I am trying to book theatre tickets for a Saturday family outing. More significantly, I can know (with ordinary certainty) that Jesus was born in the first century, that he died under Pontius Pilate and that thousands of Christians claimed he rose from the dead and have died for holding to this belief. These are simple, "common ground" facts.

At this point it is easy to make a false move and accuse me of being arrogant in claiming absolute knowledge. I am not saying I know *absolutely* everything there is to be known about Jesus, but rather that we can know some things about him *truly*.

The truth and nothing but the truth, but not the whole truth

Claiming to know truly is not the same as claiming to know exhaustively and absolutely. Relativists claim that our only choice is between knowing everything absolutely or not knowing anything truly. However, this itself is not only an absolute claim, but more significantly it is a false one, despite its popularity in university English and philosophy departments. In the real world, things are much more nuanced than this relativistic view would suggest.

Pluralism, tolerance and relativism do not form a single flavour, but are distinct ingredients with varying "nutritional" value to us and to society. *Pluralism* is simply a fact we must acknowledge and eat up with our greens. *Tolerance* is a

virtue we must cultivate an appetite for, but *relativism* is an unverifiable dogma we should pick over and if necessary spit out.

One mountain – many paths?

One of the most popular images used to teach this viewpoint is the "paths up a mountain" analogy, in which various religious devotees follow their distinctive paths, unaware that others are taking different routes up the same mountain.

The Christian believes Jesus to be the only way to God and trusts that his death and resurrection provides the only way to God and eternal life.

Unknown to the Christian, another path goes up the mountain and is being climbed by a Muslim. His journey is informed by the Five Pillars of Faith which encourage confession of faith, daily prayers, almsgiving and fasting, especially during the month of Ramadan, and pilgrimage to Mecca.

Two recording angels accompany the Muslim, one recording his good deeds and the other his bad deeds. On the weight of this evidence Allah will decide whether heaven or hell awaits the traveller.

The Buddhist pilgrim on the mountain believes that everything is one. Everything is the mountain. He seeks to be released from the illusion that he is separate from the mountain. Wrong desires have created the pain and suffering that come from being caught up in this illusion; to become one with the mountain he must follow the eightfold path, which among other things encourages right thoughts, right speech and right actions.

The point of this analogy is that there is no single correct way to climb to the mountain peak. The different religious devotees have varying but equally valid experiences of God, so no one can claim that they alone are right.

An enchanting approach

The late Allan Bloom became very concerned about the corrosive effect of relativism on the thinking of his university students, but could readily see why it was so enchanting and attractive:

"The study of history and culture teaches that all the world was mad in the past; men always thought they were right, and that led to wars, persecutions, slavery, xenophobia, racism, and chauvinism. The point is not to correct the mistakes and really be right; rather it is not to think you are right at all."[1]

We need to understand and feel the attraction of relativism. It is comforting, undemanding and enchanting. The problem with most enchantments – according to the best fairy stories – is

that they render their victims helpless with amnesia or slumbering in deep sleep for a hundred years. Is it possible that this view has bewitched us and put us into a moral and spiritual stupor, rendering us incapable of feeling hungry and passionate about objective public truth?

The price of passivity

Until the late 20th century, American surgeons lobotomised the most unstable citizens to protect society. This procedure, however, removed not only excessive and dangerous passion, but also the actual spark and drive that once energised the person.

Religiously motivated friction has given western societies an interest in minimising dangerous religious passion, and relativism is the tool of choice to achieve this, but what if relativism is incapable of promoting tolerance and genuine respectful dialogue? What if it is instead lobotomising us into becoming a disinterested, dispassionate populace? Is that too high a price to pay for safety?

"'But I don't want comfort [said the noble savage]. I want God, I want poetry, I want real danger, I want

freedom, I want goodness, and I want sin.' 'In fact,' said Mustapha Mond [the controller], 'you're claiming the right to be unhappy.'"[2]

In the Wachowski brothers' film, *The Matrix*, Neo is offered a stark choice: he can choose either the comforting illusion of significance, when in reality he is plugged into a machine, being fed the mere illusion of reality, or an uncomfortable and dangerous reality, in which his human passions are aroused and he becomes a threat to himself and the system (matrix). We know instinctively that without the truth, life and society are not worth preserving. Truth is even more important than safety.

The most urgent question is whether or not relativism's analysis is true and reliable. Does relativism pass the three basic truth tests that any world view should be subject to?

1 Is it coherent?

Does relativism make basic sense? It is generally agreed that if something is self-

contradictory it can't be true. By insisting that all truth is relative and that you cannot make any absolute claims (apart from those two that all truth is relative and you cannot make any absolute truth claims), relativism immediately fails to live by its own rules. It's rather like someone saying, "I can't speak a word of English" or "All generalisations are false". Relativism's most basic claims are self-contradictory and self-destructive and so leave relativism unable to state its own position coherently.

The nature of God

If this criticism appears semantic and theoretical, let's give relativism a chance to do better by assessing actual truth claims. Take the central claim of Christianity, Islam and Judaism that there is only one God, and put that alongside the Hindu assertion that there are two hundred and fifty million gods and then ponder the teaching of classical Buddhism that there is no God. Who is right? The relativist position is that Buddhism, Islam, Christianity, Judaism and Hinduism are all equally correct in their contradictory beliefs.

A matter of heaven

Buddhism suggests that one day a form of cosmic annihilation will take place to achieve "heaven" or "nirvana". This necessitates the destruction of all physical entities including people. When the "Atman" is subsumed into the "Brahman" we all become a drop in the ocean of everythingness. All is one and one is all.

By contrast, Islam and Christianity and some forms of Judaism believe that heaven is a real place in which we will have conscious individual existence.

A useful and trustworthy world view should help us to engage meaningfully with these religious truth claims. Relativism does not. Rather, it insists that all these beliefs are true, which is like saying that a square is the same shape as a circle and that white and black, solid and liquid, tree and tortoise are all the same.

The person of Jesus

Maybe relativism can do better when comparing more similar religions on less abstract subjects. If we compare the teachings of two of the world's monotheistic religions, Islam and Christianity, on the historical person of Jesus of Nazareth, we can give relativism a better chance of avoiding the charge of incoherence.

The Christian Scriptures are unequivocal in claiming that Jesus was the Son of God and that he died for our sins and then rose from the dead. The Koran is equally clear that Jesus is not God's Son (he is simply a prophet), Jesus did not even die (let alone for our sins) and certainly did not rise from the dead.

All relativism can do is say that Christianity and Islam are both right in their own way: "Jesus is and is not the Son of God; Jesus did and did not die and he did and did not rise from the dead." If relativism were not so outrageous in its complacency and disrespect of clearly held beliefs, it might be amusing to see how many contradictory truths could be relativised at the same time. Relativism at this point drifts dangerously towards a patronising view of race and creed by implying that Muslims can't help believing what they do; it is simply down to their ethnicity and upbringing. Christianity, by contrast, is willing to take the Islamic view of Jesus seriously and to examine the historical records to see which position makes more sense of the available evidence.

Tolerance versus indifference

Tolerance is surely only possible when both Christians and Muslims take each other's claims seriously and acknowledge these profound differences. Without disagreement there can be nothing to tolerate. The relativistic approach simply trivialises these differences with a pompous declaration of "whatever", and substitutes a corrosive and patronising indifference for genuine tolerance.

2 Does it hook up with reality?

The second test is sometimes called the test for correspondence. Does relativism describe things as they really are? Do its claims correspond to other things we know to be true?

We are happy to acknowledge that things like clothes, football teams and music are in the realm of taste and opinion. In the world of aesthetics and art, we may concede that beauty is largely in the eye of the beholder, although the art critic Brian Sewell once commented on the remarkable achievement of some contemporary artists in producing work that even the artist's mother would dislike.

At the same time, however, much of our lives operate on absolutes. We do not want our doctors, scientists and bank managers to be relativistic about medicine, measurements and money. While we could be fairly indifferent if someone believed that pain is relative

and all in the mind, it would be another matter if that person was your surgeon and suggested operating on you without anaesthetic. Neither do we mind our bank managers being relaxed in their personal view of money so long as they are objective and accurate about the money we have deposited in their bank.

One way

Muhammad recited a way, the Buddha discovered a way; but Jesus uniquely said: **"I am the way, the truth and the life. No one comes to the Father except through me"** (John 14:6, NIV). **"I am the door; whoever enters through me will be saved"** (John 10:9, NIV). If Christianity appears arrogant, it is probably because Jesus' claims cannot be relativised. Jesus received worship, forgave people their sin, claimed to be the Judge of all people and even took the "I Am" title of God for himself.[3] Now if you are thinking that this was all somehow more acceptable to a 1st-century audience made up of Jewish and Roman citizens than it is to us, you are forgetting two things: first, the Roman Empire encouraged its own pluralistic mix of religious beliefs and reacted violently to Christians who consistently refused to worship Caesar as a god. Secondly, the Jewish leaders who heard Jesus make these claims were so enraged by his blasphemy they made several attempts on his life before persuading the Romans to crucify him. In short, if we are to make an authentic and meaningful response to Jesus, we have to engage with what he claimed and come to reasonable conclusions based on the available evidence.

Both G K Chesterton and C S Lewis became persuaded by who Jesus was when they explored the only real options left open to them. Lewis summarises this process:

"I am trying here to prevent anyone saying the really foolish thing that people often say about him: 'I am ready to accept Jesus as a great moral teacher, but I don't accept his claim to be God.' That is the one

thing we must not say. A man who was merely a man and said the sort of things Jesus said would not be a great moral teacher. He would either be a lunatic – on the level with the man who says he is a poached egg – or else he would be the devil of hell. You must make your choice. Either this man was ... the Son of God: or else a madman or something worse."[4]

Bad, mad or God?

We cannot intelligently put Jesus into the "good man", "Teacher" or "Prophet" category. There are only three options open to us. Option one is that Jesus was bad. According to this view, in claiming to be God, Jesus actually knew his claim was false. That makes him the biggest liar and manipulator of all time, a monstrous deceiver who makes the death-cult leader Jim Jones seem moderate. If Jesus knew that his claim to be God was false, he was not only a liar but also a hypocrite since he demanded a level of honesty and transparency in his followers that has never been surpassed. Is it really likely that the source of such unrivalled honesty and integrity is a hypocritical liar? Even worse is Jesus' claim that his followers' eternal destiny (heaven or hell) depended entirely on their believing that he was the Christ who could forgive their sins and would judge the world.

"The hypothesis of imposture is so revolting to moral as well as common sense, that its mere statement is its condemnation ... no scholar of any decency and self-respect would now dare to profess it openly. How, in the name of logic, common-sense, and experience, could an impostor – that is a deceitful, selfish, depraved man – have invented, and consistently maintained from the beginning to end, the purest noblest character known in history with the most perfect air of truth and reality?"[5]

In rejecting the option that Jesus knew his claims were false we are left with only two alternatives. Either Jesus was deluded or he was who he claimed to be.

Mad?

At first glance the option that Jesus was mad sounds much more plausible than the preposterous notion of him being a megalomaniacal liar. This option quickly loses credibility, however, when you consider Jesus' culture and environment. He was brought up on a strict belief that there was only one God, who alone could forgive sins and receive worship. For a Jew in 1st-century Palestine to believe he had the authority to forgive sin, receive worship and subject the whole world to judgement on the last day, he would be the victim of a deep clinical delusion of the most disturbing and extreme nature.

"The charge of an extravagant, self-deluding enthusiasm is the last to be fastened on Jesus. Where can we find the traces of it in his history? Do we detect them in the calm authority of his precepts? in the mild, practical and beneficent spirit of his religion ...? ... The truth is, that, remarkable as the character of Jesus was, it was

distinguished by nothing more than by calmness and self-possession."[6]

God?

Accepting the third option that Jesus is exactly who he claims to be is the only way to make sense of him and his legacy. Even though Jesus never wrote a book or led an army, more books have been written about him than any person who walked our planet, and millions more people follow him than anyone else alive or dead. Jesus is simply too big and uncompromising to relativise away. His claim to be the only One who could bring us forgiveness and a restored relationship with God must be taken seriously and weighed carefully.

3 Is relativism useful and good for society?

Relativism as a world view not only contradicts itself, but it also fails to correspond to the reality that there are truths or "givens" around which we order much of our lives. The third and final test is the pragmatic test: is relativism useful and beneficial to society?

The most notorious monument to moral relativism is Hitler's final solution. Emboldened by Nietzsche's teaching in which God and therefore all absolutes are dead, Hitler exercised his freedom from absolute truth and created the final solution.

"When one gives up Christian belief one thereby deprives oneself of the *right* to Christian morality. For the latter is absolutely not self-evident: one must make this point clear again and again ..., If Christianity is a system, a consistently thought out and *complete* view of things. If one breaks out of it a fundamental idea, the belief in God, one thereby breaks the whole thing to pieces: one has nothing of any consequence left in one's hands."[7]

The New Atheists would like to avoid Nietzsche's conclusion but have nowhere to go. In an early interview Richard

Dawkins expressed a view that he has repeated many times in different forms:

"I couldn't, ultimately, argue intellectually against somebody who did something I found obnoxious. I think I could finally only say, 'Well, in this society you can't get away with it' and call the police."[8]

What if Dawkins did not find the behaviour obnoxious? What if society did not? What if the police did not? Who defines "obnoxiousness" anyway?

The arrogance of relativism

Why have we let this view on board? What relativism declares at Customs is that it is one view among many and is worthy of consideration alongside the others, but what it smuggles through is that it is the only true approach and all other views are judged by it. Far from regarding itself as merely a product of secular western society, it sees itself standing alone as timelessly true.

We have been conned. With this insight, let us go back to the image of the mountain paths. Where is the relativist in this image? He is at the top of the mountain; it is he – not Allah or Jesus – waiting to greet all those sincerely deluded worshippers. We must wake ourselves up from an enchantment that has duped us into embracing a view that is not only incoherent and patronising but deeply corrosive to the religious and moral fibre of society. The real arrogance of this view is that it shuts down genuine thought and inquiry and allows us to sleepwalk up the mountain on any path we choose, offering us the certain assurance that we are all on the right road.

Scaling the summit

Do all mountain paths lead to the summit? Not the ones I've climbed. Some paths lead to dead ends and others lead to danger. To be lost on a mountain ultimately means we will perish.

"For God so loved the world that he gave his one and only Son, that whoever believes in him shall not perish, but have eternal life" (John 3:16, NIV). If Jesus is who he claims to be – the way to God, the revealer of truth about sin, heaven and hell – we must take him seriously. Regardless of our religious upbringing, says Jesus, we are all heading in the wrong direction unless we are following him. For it is only in Jesus that God took on human form and broke into history as a man. It is in no one else but Jesus that human sin and rebellion were dealt with and punished. Jesus died on the cross to take the punishment that your rebellion and mine deserved. As a man Jesus adequately represented us and as God was able to deal with our sin and defeat death by rising out of his tomb. The death and resurrection of Jesus cannot be relativised away any more than his claims can be; the empty tomb cannot have been relatively empty.

Even though we may continue to struggle with the implications of Jesus being the only way to God, we must however concede that it would be arrogant of us not to take his claims, his death and his resurrection seriously. You may still wish to keep an open mind about who you think Jesus is. Open-mindedness is to be commended wherever it is found, so long as you realise that the purpose of an open mind is the same as that of an open mouth: to close it again on something solid. The danger with keeping your mind permanently open is that after a while it is not easy to keep truth in it and error out of it. This state of intellectual lockjaw can degenerate into a confusion of truth with error and goodness with evil. By contrast, Jesus said, **"If you hold to my teaching, you are really my followers. Then you will know the truth, and the truth will set you free"** (see John 8:31-32).

Your response

If you would like to investigate further the key evidence for Christianity visit www.bethinking.org/booklets and choose from a variety of talks and articles.

If you have already reached the conclusion that Jesus is who he claims to be then you will find yourself with a decision to make, namely whether you will accept him or reject him as Lord. To reject Jesus' lordship you need do nothing. But to accept, you must come to him on his terms: being willing to turn away from being independent of God and asking him, by virtue of his death and resurrection, to forgive you and bring you into a restored relationship with God.

You can be confident, because of who Jesus is and what he has done, that if you sincerely repent of going your own way and pray to God for forgiveness and ask him to make you a follower of Jesus, he will hear your prayer.

Prayer

Dear God, I admit that I have lived independently of you and have offended your love and provoked your anger with my proud, selfish attitude to you and all that you have made.

I thank you that in Jesus I can be sure you took on human form and broke into history as a man. I accept that it was only in Jesus that human sin and rebellion were dealt with and punished. Thank you that Jesus died in my place, bearing the punishment my sin deserves.

I now turn away from everything that is wrong in my life and ask you to forgive me by virtue of who Jesus is and what he achieved on the cross. Please send the Spirit of Jesus to live in me, to renew me and help me to be a follower of Jesus from this day on and for the rest of my life. Amen.

If you have prayed this prayer, speak to a Christian friend or go to our website www.bethinking.org/booklets and email us using "Contact us".

Footnotes

1   Allan Bloom, *Closing of the American Mind* (New York: Simon & Schuster, 1987, page 26).

2   Aldous Huxley, *Brave New World* (New York: Harper & Brothers, 1932, chapter 17).

3   Jesus' claims to be God: Matthew 27:43; Mark 14:61-64; Luke 20:41-44; Luke 21:27; John 8:57-58; John 10:30.

4   C S Lewis, *Mere Christianity* (London: Collins, 1952, pages 40-41).

5   Philip Schaff [a Christian historian], *The Person of Christ*, quoted in Josh McDowell, *The New Evidence that Demands a Verdict* (Nashville: Nelson, 1999, page 160).

6   William Channing [a Unitarian writer], quoted in *The New Evidence that Demands a Verdict* (Nashville: Nelson, 1999, pages 161-2).

7   Friedrich Wilhelm Nietzsche, *Twilight of the Idols* (London: Penguin, 1990, page 80, emphasis in original).

8   From an interview with Nick Pollard, *The Space-Time Gazette*, Autumn 1995.